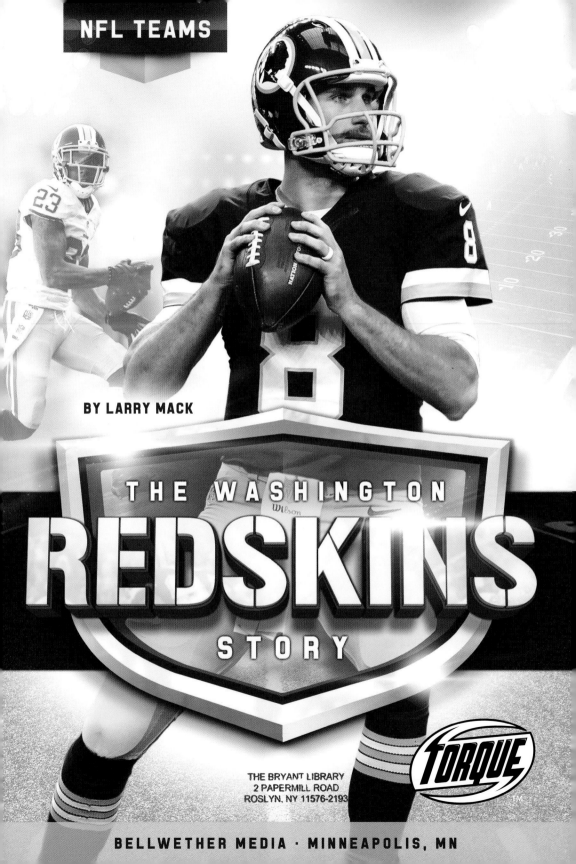

BY LARRY MACK

THE WASHINGTON
REDSKINS
STORY

TORQUE

BELLWETHER MEDIA · MINNEAPOLIS, MN

Are you ready to take it to the extreme? Torque books thrust you into the action-packed world of sports, vehicles, mystery, and adventure. These books may include dirt, smoke, fire, and chilling tales. **WARNING**: read at your own risk.

This edition first published in 2017 by Bellwether Media, Inc.

No part of this publication may be reproduced in whole or in part without written permission of the publisher. For information regarding permission, write to Bellwether Media, Inc., Attention: Permissions Department, 5357 Penn Avenue South, Minneapolis, MN 55419.

Library of Congress Cataloging-in-Publication Data

Names: Mack, Larry, author.
Title: The Washington Redskins Story / by Larry Mack.
Description: Minneapolis, MN : Bellwether Media, Inc., 2017. | Series:
   Torque: NFL Teams | Includes index.
Identifiers: LCCN 2015043382 | ISBN 9781626173866 (hardcover : alk. paper)
Subjects: LCSH: Washington Redskins (Football team)–History–Juvenile literature.
Classification: LCC GV956.W3 M3 2017 | DDC 796.332/6409753–dc23
LC record available at http://lccn.loc.gov/2015043382

Printed in the United States of America, North Mankato, MN.

TABLE OF CONTENTS

It is the last game of the 2015 season. The Washington Redskins are in Dallas to face their longtime **rival**, the Cowboys.

Kirk Cousins

Jamison Crowder

At the end of the first quarter, **quarterback** Kirk Cousins has the Redskins up by three touchdowns! But the Cowboys come back with touchdowns in the second quarter.

Colt McCoy

Before halftime, backup quarterback Colt McCoy replaces Cousins. The Redskins want to rest Cousins.

The plan works. In the fourth quarter, McCoy connects with **wide receiver** Rashad Ross for another touchdown. It is Washington's day. They are in the **playoffs**!

SCORING TERMS

END ZONE

the area at each end of a football field; a team scores by entering the opponent's end zone with the football.

EXTRA POINT

a score that occurs when a kicker kicks the ball between the opponent's goal posts after a touchdown is scored; 1 point.

FIELD GOAL

a score that occurs when a kicker kicks the ball between the opponent's goal posts; 3 points.

SAFETY

a score that occurs when a player on offense is tackled behind his own goal line; 2 points for defense.

TOUCHDOWN

a score that occurs when a team crosses into its opponent's end zone with the football; 6 points.

TWO-POINT CONVERSION

a score that occurs when a team crosses into its opponent's end zone with the football after scoring a touchdown; 2 points.

Rashad Ross

The Washington Redskins are a National
Football League (NFL) team with a fighting spirit.
They have fought their way to the playoffs more
than 20 times. They have even won titles.

The team has also pushed for new NFL traditions. They were among the first to show all their games on TV!

The Redskins' home is FedExField in Landover, Maryland. It is just outside Washington, D.C. The team has played in this stadium since 1997.

FedExField had an energy makeover in 2011. More than 8,000 **solar panels** were added. They give power to the whole stadium on non-game days!

THE DISTRICT

The "D.C." after Washington stands for District of Columbia. This is the home of the nation's government.

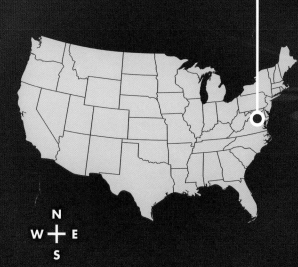

LANDOVER, MARYLAND

N
W ✛ E
S

The Redskins are a National Football **Conference** (NFC) team. Their main East **Division** rival is the Cowboys. These two teams have met more than 100 times since 1960.

The Redskins' two other division rivals are from nearby states. The Giants are from New York. The Eagles are from Pennsylvania.

NFL DIVISIONS

AFC

AFC NORTH

BALTIMORE **RAVENS**	CINCINNATI **BENGALS**
CLEVELAND **BROWNS**	PITTSBURGH **STEELERS**

AFC EAST

BUFFALO **BILLS**	MIAMI **DOLPHINS**
NEW ENGLAND **PATRIOTS**	NEW YORK **JETS**

AFC SOUTH

HOUSTON **TEXANS**	INDIANAPOLIS **COLTS**
JACKSONVILLE **JAGUARS**	TENNESSEE **TITANS**

AFC WEST

DENVER **BRONCOS**	KANSAS CITY **CHIEFS**
OAKLAND **RAIDERS**	SAN DIEGO **CHARGERS**

NFC

NFC NORTH

CHICAGO
BEARS

DETROIT
LIONS

GREEN BAY
PACKERS

MINNESOTA
VIKINGS

NFC EAST

DALLAS
COWBOYS

NEW YORK
GIANTS

PHILADELPHIA
EAGLES

WASHINGTON
REDSKINS

NFC SOUTH

ATLANTA
FALCONS

CAROLINA
PANTHERS

NEW ORLEANS
SAINTS

TAMPA BAY
BUCCANEERS

NFC WEST

ARIZONA
CARDINALS

LOS ANGELES
RAMS

SAN FRANCISCO
49ERS

SEATTLE
SEAHAWKS

The Redskins spent their first five seasons in Boston, Massachusetts. In their first year, they were called the Braves.

The team moved to Washington, D.C., in 1937. That same year, they won the NFL Championship. Then they won it all again in 1942.

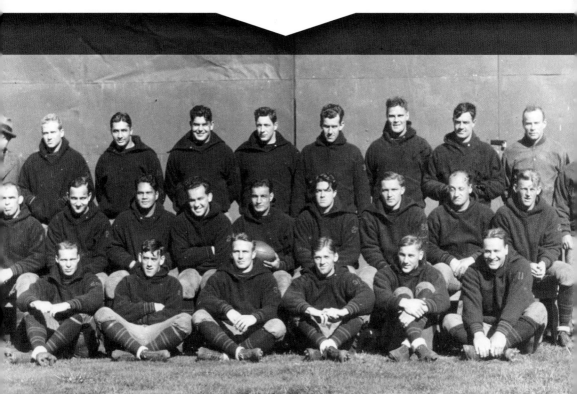

Boston Braves, 1932 season

REDSKINS 14
WIN - 6

In 1946, the Redskins started a **slump**. Then they turned things around in the 1970s. The team made it to **Super Bowl** 7. But they could not pull off a win.

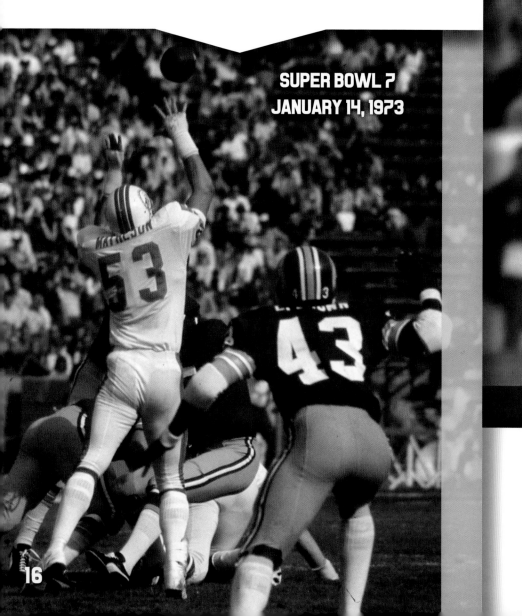

SUPER BOWL 7
JANUARY 14, 1973

In 1983, the Redskins finally won a Super Bowl. They repeated in 1988 and 1992.

REDSKINS
TIMELINE

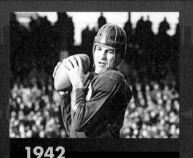

1932

Formed as the Boston Braves; renamed the Redskins the next year.

1937

Moved to Washington, D.C.

1942

Won their second NFL Championship, beating the Chicago Bears (14-6)

1937

Won their first NFL Championship, beating the Chicago Bears (28-21)

1972

Won the NFC Championship game, beating the Dallas Cowboys (26-3)

1983

Won Super Bowl 17,
beating the Miami Dolphins

27 FINAL SCORE **17**

1992

Won Super Bowl 26,
beating the Buffalo Bills

37 FINAL SCORE **24**

1984

Won the NFC
Championship
game, beating
the San Francisco
49ers (24-21)

1988

Won Super Bowl 22,
beating the Denver Broncos

42 FINAL SCORE **10**

2004

Earned 500th
all-time victory,
beating the
Tampa Bay
Buccaneers
(16-10)

Several star quarterbacks have worn a Redskins jersey. Sammy Baugh helped the team win the 1937 NFL Championship. He was just a **rookie** at the time.

SUPER RECORD-SETTER

In 1988, Doug Williams made history. He became the first African-American quarterback to start a Super Bowl.

Joe Theismann

Joe Theismann led the Redskins to their first Super Bowl victory. He became the team's top passer ever. One of his favorite receivers was Hall-of-Famer Art Monk.

During the Super Bowl years, the hardworking **offensive line** was nicknamed "The Hogs." Hall-of-Fame **guard** Russ Grimm was an original hog.

Cornerback Darrell Green helped the **defense** in Super Bowls 22 and 26. He played 20 seasons in a row for Washington!

TEAM GREATS

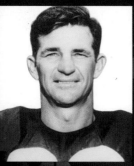

SAMMY BAUGH
QUARTERBACK,
DEFENSIVE BACK, PUNTER
1937-1952

JOE THEISMANN
QUARTERBACK
1974-1985

ART MONK
WIDE RECEIVER
1980-1993

A NEW HOG?

Today, tackle Trent Williams is the protector of the quarterback.

RUSS GRIMM
GUARD
1981-1991

DARRELL GREEN
CORNERBACK
1983-2002

TRENT WILLIAMS
OFFENSIVE TACKLE
2010-PRESENT

The Hogettes

The Redskins have some loyal fans. One group of men was known as "The Hogettes." They wore dresses, wigs, and plastic pig noses to games for 30 years.

The Hail BBQ Crew hosts a large **tailgate** outside before home games. Fans eat grilled food and toss footballs around.

Redskins fans rally with song. "Hail to the Redskins" has been a longtime fight song. The team's marching band first performed it in 1938.

With great football and fun, it is no wonder the Redskins sell out FedExField. They have sold out every home game since 1968!

MORE ABOUT THE
REDSKINS

Team name:
Washington Redskins

Team name explained:
Named after Native American warriors (Some worry that the name is not respectful and want it changed.)

Nickname: The Hogs

Joined NFL: 1932

Conference: **NFC**

Division: **East**

Main rivals: **Dallas Cowboys, New York Giants**

Hometown:
Washington, D.C.
(Landover, Maryland)

Training camp location: Bon Secours Washington Redskins Training Center, Richmond, Virginia

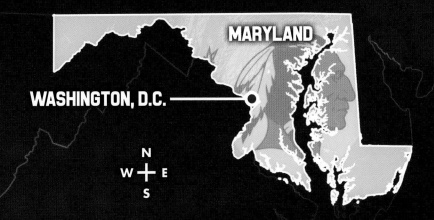

Home stadium name: FedExField

Stadium opened: 1997

Seats in stadium: 82,000

Logo: Profile of a Native American

Colors: Burgundy, white, gold

GLOSSARY

conference—a large grouping of sports teams that often play one another

cornerback—a player on defense whose main job is to stop wide receivers from catching passes; a cornerback is positioned outside of the linebackers.

defense—the group of players who try to stop the opposing team from scoring

division—a small grouping of sports teams that often play one another; usually there are several divisions of teams in a conference.

guard—a player on offense whose job is to tackle the linemen of the opposing team

offensive line—players on offense whose main jobs are to protect the quarterback and to block for running backs

playoffs—the games played after the regular NFL season is over; playoff games determine which teams play in the Super Bowl.

quarterback—a player on offense whose main job is to throw and hand off the ball

rival—a long-standing opponent

rookie—a first-year player in a sports league

slump—a period of time during which a team has difficulty winning

solar panels—flat panels that use the sun's light or heat to create power

Super Bowl—the championship game for the NFL

tailgate—a cookout in the parking lot at a sporting event; a tailgate is also the door at the back of a pickup truck that flips down.

wide receiver—a player on offense whose main job is to catch passes from the quarterback

TO LEARN MORE

AT THE LIBRARY

Frisch, Aaron. *Washington Redskins*. Mankato, Minn.: Creative Education, 2014.

Gilbert, Sara. *The Story of the Washington Redskins*. Mankato, Minn.: Creative Education, 2014.

Temple, Ramey. *Washington Redskins*. New York, N.Y.: AV2 by Weigl, 2015.

ON THE WEB

Learning more about the Washington Redskins is as easy as 1, 2, 3.

1. Go to www.factsurfer.com.

2. Enter "Washington Redskins" into the search box.

3. Click the "Surf" button and you will see a list of related web sites.

With factsurfer.com, finding more information is just a click away.

INDEX